Earth and Its Moon

Chris Oxlade

rosen publishing's
rosen central

New York

Published in 2008 by The Rosen Publishing Group, Inc.
29 East 21st Street, New York, NY 10010

Copyright © 2008 Wayland/The Rosen Publishing Group, Inc.

All rights reserved. No part of this book may be reproduced in any form
without permission in writing from the publisher, except by a reviewer.

First Edition

Editor: Nicola Edwards
Designer: Tim Mayer
Consultant: Ian Graham

The right of Chris Oxlade to be identified as the author of this work has been asserted by him in accordan
with the Copyright, Designs, and Patents Act, 1988.

Cover: The Earth and its Moon are partners in space, but they are two very different worlds.

Photo credits: James L. Amos/Corbis 23c. Stuart Baines/Ecoscene: 17t, 17b, 37t. Andrew Brown/Ecoscene: 18
Lloyd Cuff/Corbis; 9. Christian Darkin/SPL: 22. ESA: 24b. ESA/CNES/ARIANESPACE-Service Optique CSG: 40.
Macduff Everton/Corbis: 14. Chinch Gryniewicz/Ecoscene: 27. GSFC/NASA: 13t, 15t. F. Hasler, M. Jentoff-Nils
H. Pierce, K. Palaniappan & M. Manyin/GSFC/NASA: 10. Andy Hibbert/Ecoscene: 23b. HSTI/NASA: 20. Georg
Huey/Corbis: 11. JPL/NASA: 1, 4, 5, 32, 41. JSC/NASA: 28, 29, 30, 45. Frank Lukassek/zefa/Corbis: 34. David
Malin Images/Anglo-Australian Observatory: 7. John & Lisa Merrill/Corbis: 39. NASA: 6, 35. NASA/SPL: 16,
44. Graham Neden/Corbis: 12. Patrick Pleul/epa/Corbis: 36. Jose Fuste Raga/Corbis: 21. Detlev van
Ravenswaay/SPL: 31. Roger Ressmeyer/Corbis: 38. Reuters/Corbis: 8, 25c. Ria/Novosti/SPL: 33b. Erik
Schaffer/Ecoscene: 25. Superstock: front cover. © Joe Tucciarone: 26. Ralph White/ Corbis: 43. Jim
Winkley/Ecoscene: 42.

Library of Congress Cataloging-in-Publication Data

Olxade, Chris.
  Earth and Its moon / Chris Olxade. -- 1st ed.
    p. cm. -- (Earth and space)
  Includes index.
  ISBN-13: 978-1-4042-3734-6 (library binding)
  ISBN-10: 1-4042-3734-8 (library binding)
 1. Earth--Juvenile literature. 2. Moon--Juvenile literature. I. Title.
  QB631.4.O69 2007
  525--dc22
                            2006028332

Manufactured in China

Contents

Earth and its Moon

Our Earth seems an enormous place to us. But it is just a small member of a whole family of planets. Together with the Sun, moons, and other objects in space, these planets make up our Solar System. The Moon is Earth's companion in space.

The planets

There are eight planets in our Solar System. The four planets closest to the Sun (Mercury, Venus, Earth, and Mars: the inner planets) are rocky worlds with solid surfaces. The other four (Jupiter, Saturn, Uranus, and Neptune) are huge balls of gas. They are known as the *gas giants*. Pluto, a small, icy body beyond Neptune, was classed as a planet until 2006, when experts at the International Astronomical Union decided to downgrade it to a "dwarf planet."

Earth's special nature

Earth is largest of the inner planets. It is the only place in the Solar System where there is liquid water on the surface and where there is life. Astronomers have found planets around other stars, too, but so far, none like Earth. Earth's blue oceans and green vegetation make it look very different from the other planets. We know it as the "Blue Planet."

From top to bottom, the planets (not to scale) are Mercury, Venus, Earth, Mars, Jupiter, Saturn, Uranus, and Neptune.

e Moon

Moon is the only natural object that orbits (moves
und) Earth. It is about one third the width of Earth,
approximately 240,000 miles (385,000 kilometers)
ay. It is much larger than most of the moons in the
ar System. Some astronomers think of Earth and
on as a double planet. The Moon is a very different
rld from Earth. It is covered with craters and dark
ions called *seas*. There is no liquid water here, no
osphere, and no life.

How do we know?

Walking on the Moon

The Moon is the only object
(apart from Earth) that humans
have visited. U.S. astronauts flew a
series of missions to the Moon in
the Apollo spacecraft, starting in
1969. The astronauts carried out
experiments and brought back
samples of Moon rock. The last
visit was in 1972. Nobody has
been to the Moon since,
mainly because the cost
is huge.

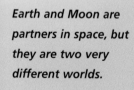

Earth and Moon are
partners in space, but
they are two very
different worlds.

Moving Through Space

Earth moves around the Sun in a path called an orbit, always staying about 93 million miles (150 million km) from the Sun. The orbit is the shape of a slightly squashed circle. The Moon orbits Earth, remaining about 240,000 miles (385,000 km) away from it.

Spinning worlds

Earth and Moon spin around as they move along their orbits. Earth spins around its axis, which is an imaginary line through Earth. Earth's poles are where this line sticks through the surface. Earth's spin causes night and day to happen. As part of the world faces the Sun, it has day. As it faces away from the Sun, it is in Earth's shadow and has night. The Earth completes one spin every day.

Earth's spin also makes the Sun, Moon, and stars appear to move across the sky as the day and night pass by. They don't really move. Earth's spin means that you move in a giant circle once a day. It is like sitting on a spinning merry-go-round and seeing the fairground its in appear to move around you.

One side of Earth by the Sun, seen fr the Moon as it orb the Earth.

The Moon also spins as it orbits Earth. But it spins very slowly compared to the Earth. In fact, it completes exactly one spin during each orbit. This means that the same side of the Moon faces Earth all the time.

SPACE DATA

Earth and Moon

Distance from Earth to Sun:	93 million mi. (149.6 million km)
Distance from Earth to Moon:	238,330 mi. (384,400 km)
Earth: time for one spin:	23 hours, 56 minutes
Moon: time for one spin:	27.3 Earth days
Earth year:	365.26 days
Lunar month:	29.5 Earth days

is photograph was en over several urs. The lines are r trails made by th's spin.

Days, months, and years

The movements of Earth and Moon give us days, years, and months. A day is the time it takes Earth to complete one spin. A year is the time it takes Earth to complete one orbit of the Sun. A lunar month is the time between one New Moon and the next.

Gravity

The force of gravity keeps Earth and Moon in orbit. Gravity attracts Earth to the Sun, and the Moon to Earth. It acts like a string, stopping Earth and Moon from flying off into space, and making them move in a circle. At the same time, because Earth and Moon are moving along their orbits, they do not fall toward the Sun or Earth.

Earth's Structure

Earth is a giant ball of rock. If you could dig a hole straight dow to the center of Earth, you would find four different layers of rc The surface we stand on is solid, but not many miles under our there is runny, partly molten rock. T makes the surface rocks move abou and causes earthquakes and volcanc

Layers of Earth

The first layer of Earth is the crust. Under Earth's continents, the crust is an average of 22 miles (35 kilometer thick. But it is only a few miles thick under the oceans. Under the crust is a layer of rock almost 1,860 miles (3,000 kilometers) thick, called the *mantle*. It makes up about three-quarters of Earth. Just under the cru the mantle is so hot that its rock is partly molten.

Under the mantle is Earth's core, wh is about 4,340 miles (7,000 kilometer across. The core is made mostly of ir It has two layers—a solid inner core a molten outer core.

Powerful seismic waves traveling across Earth's surface can cause damage such as this, in Kobe, Japan.

How do we know?

Seismic waves

A seismic wave is a wave that moves through Earth's rock. Seismic waves are caused by earthquakes. The waves spread through Earth from where the earthquake happens. They bounce or change direction when they hit a boundary between different layers of rock. Studying where waves arrive at Earth's surface after earthquakes has allowed geologists to detec the layers deep inside the Earth.

SPACE DATA

Earth

Diameter:	7,909 mi. (12,756 km)
Mass:	6,600 billion billion tons
Density:	4.6 tons per cubic yard (5.5 tonnes/cubic meter)
Temperature in center of core:	8,132°F (4,500°C)
Average surface temperature:	59°F (15°C)

*giant crack is called the San Andreas fault. It is
⋅re two tectonic plates meet in California.*

A cracked crust

Earth's crust is cracked into giant pieces called *tectonic plates.* Slow-moving molten rock in the mantle makes the plates move very slowly. This movement is called *continental drift.* In some places, the edges of the plates are moving apart. In others, they slide past each other. Sometimes the edges of plates collide with each other. Earthquakes happen when the moving plates become jammed and then move suddenly. As far as we know, Earth is the only planet with these tectonic plates.

Earth's Surface

From space, Earth looks very different from the other planets in Solar System. Astronauts are the only people lucky enough to se Earth from space. From the photographs they send back, we can see a surface that is made up of blue water, green vegetation, brown rock and soil, and white ice.

Water

Two-thirds of Earth's surface is covered with oceans. The largest ocean, the Pacific, covers almost half of the globe. The ocea are thousands of feet deep. They contai 97 percent of all Earth's water. One percent of the water is in lakes and rivers, and in underground rocks. The other 2 percent is in the form of ice, mountain glaciers, and in thick ice sheets at the poles.

Land masses

Land covers about a third of Earth's surface. The landscape is made up of a wide variety of features, such as mounta ranges and flat plains. Mountain ranges, su as the Himalayas and Andes, are mostly at th boundaries between the tectonic plates, where colliding plates force up the surface rocks.

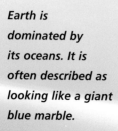

Earth is dominated by its oceans. It is often described as looking like a giant blue marble.

Earth Facts

Earth's features

● The highest point on Earth is the summit of Mount Everest, 29,029 ft. (8,848 m) above sea level.

● The lowest point on Earth is the bottom of the Marianas Trench, in the Pacific Ocean, 35,840 ft. (10,924 m) below sea level.

Earth has hundreds of active volcanoes, which also build mountains. Most volcanoes are at the plate boundaries, where molten rock pushes its way to the surface.

Water features

Earth has deep canyons and valleys that have been cut by flowing rivers and glaciers. Alongside the rivers are wide plains, and at their ends, where they meet the sea, are deltas. River basins are huge areas that are drained by a system of rivers. At the coasts are cliffs and beaches.

Islands

Grand Canyon in
ona was cut over
ons of years by
flowing water of
Colorado River.

Dotted in the oceans are islands. Some islands are actually part of the continents. The land is separated from the rest of the continent when the sea level rises. Islands far out in the oceans, such as the Hawaiian Islands, are usually the tops of giant undersea volcanoes.

The Atmosphere

The atmosphere is a layer of air that surrounds Earth. It is very thin compared to Earth, like the skin on an apple. Moving upward, the atmosphere gradually gets thinner and thinner, until it ends a few hundred miles up.

Gases of the atmosphere

The two main gases in atmosphere are nitrogen and oxygen, which is the gas we need to breathe. Nitrogen makes up 78 percent of the air, and oxygen 20 percent. The remaining 2 percent is made up of many different gases, including carbon dioxide. There is always some water vapor in the atmosphere, too. A special form of oxygen, called *ozone*, exists in the upper atmosphere. The ozone layer stops much of the harmful ultraviolet radiation that comes from the Sun from reaching Earth's surface.

Weather balloons carry instruments into the atmosphe to measure things, such as temperatu and pressure at different altitudes.

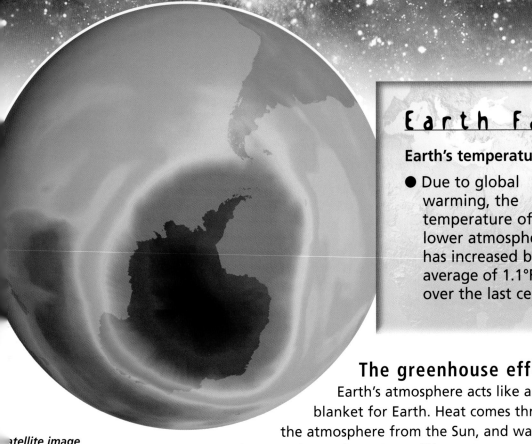

Satellite image showing the "ozone hole" over the Antarctic.

Earth's temperature

● Due to global warming, the temperature of Earth's lower atmosphere has increased by an average of 1.1°F (0.6°C) over the last century.

The greenhouse effect

Earth's atmosphere acts like a blanket for Earth. Heat comes through the atmosphere from the Sun, and warms the surface. Earth's surface gives off heat. Some gases in the atmosphere trap this heat, warming the atmosphere. The gases that trap most heat are carbon dioxide and methane. This effect is called the *greenhouse effect* because glass in a greenhouse traps heat in a similar way.

Threats to the atmosphere

In the last 200 years, we have added gases to the atmosphere that are changing how the atmosphere works. For example, chemicals called CFCs, used in fridges and freezers, have caused a hole in the ozone layer. Carbon dioxide from burning fuels is increasing the greenhouse effect, making the atmosphere warmer. This is known as *global warming*. Most scientists agree that global warming is changing the world's climates.

How do we know?
Measuring the atmosphere

We know about the atmosphere from measurements and observations from Earth and from space. Measurements of the atmosphere, such as the air pressure, temperature, and concentration of different gases, are taken by aircraft and by instruments carried by weather balloons. Satellites observe the atmosphere from above.

Earth's Weather

The weather that happens on Earth is driven by the Sun. The Sun's heat warms Earth's surface, and the warm surface heats the air above it. This heat makes winds blow and clouds form, causing giant swirling weather systems that are visible from space.

Rising and falling air

The Sun's heat warms some parts of Earth's surface more than others. The surface is heated more where the Sun shines from high in the sky and less where the Sun's rays hit at a low angle. Bare soil also heats up more than land covered with plants and the oceans.

Where the surface is warmed up, it heats the air above it. This makes the air expand. The air becomes less dense and floats upward. Cooler air flows in sideways to replace it. This moving air creates winds. As the air moves above Earth's surface, the spinning of Earth underneath it makes the winds swirl around to form weather systems. The moving air spreads heat over Earth's surface.

Here, humid air has been heated by wa land and risen. Its water vapor has formed clouds.

some parts of the ...d, masses of giant ...understorms form into damaging weather systems ...d hurricanes (also ...wn as cyclones or typhoons).

Clouds and rain

The heat from the Sun also warms the water in the oceans and in the soil. Some of the water evaporates, turning into a gas called water vapor. This warm, humid air rises upward. As it does, it cools. This makes the water vapor condense. It turns to tiny drops of water. Billions of these drops form clouds. If the drops become large enough, they fall back to the surface as rain.

The water cycle

When rain falls to the ground, some soaks in. The rest runs across the surface and collects in streams and rivers. The water in the rivers flows down to the sea. Some of it then evaporates to form new clouds and rain. Some of the water in the soil and on the ground evaporates and goes back into the air, too. So water circulates between the oceans, the atmosphere, and the land. This is called the *water cycle*. It carries water across the land masses, allowing life to survive.

SPACE DATA

Extreme weather records

Highest temperature:	136°F (58°C) (Libya)
Lowest temperature:	-128°F (-89°C) (Antarctica)
Fastest wind:	230 mph (371 kph) (Mount Washington)
Heaviest rain:	1.5 in. (38.1 mm) in a minute (Guadeloupe)

Climates and Seasons

The pattern of weather a place on Earth has is called a *climate*. Different places on Earth have different climates. In some places, it is freezing cold all year-round. In others, it is hot and rainy all year. Many places have seasons, with different weather at different times of year.

Climate zones

The climate that a place has depends mainly on how far it is from the equator (an imaginary line around the middle of Earth). Close to the equator, the Sun shines from high overhead all year. There is also high rainfall most of the year. This is a tropical climate. Close to Earth's poles, the Sun's rays hit at a very low angle. The snow and ice also reflect the heat. So here it is extremely cold all year. This is a polar climate. Between the equator and the poles, many places have cool winters and warm summers. This is a temperate climate. In some places on Earth, it is very dry all year. This is an arid climate. The climate a place has also depends on how close it is to the oceans, and how high up it is.

The kind of vegetation in a place is closely linked to the climate. In polar climates, it is too cold for plants to grow, and the ground is covered with snow and ice. In very arid climates, it is too dry, and so there are brown deserts. In tropical climates, there is dense rain forest. And in temperate climates, there are forests of deciduous and coniferous trees.

A map of daytime temperatures show that the equator i heated more than polar regions.

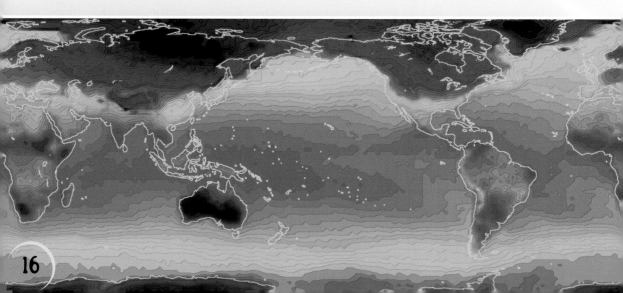

What causes seasons

Seasons happen because Earth's axis is tilted over to one side. A place has summer when the pole it is nearest to is tilted toward the Sun. On the opposite side of the orbit, this pole is tilted away from the Sun. Then it gets less heat, and it is winter. When it is summer in the northern hemisphere, it is winter in the southern hemisphere, and vice versa. The tilt also means that there are more hours of sunshine in the summer than in the winter. During midsummer, places near Earth's poles have daylight 24 hours a day. During midwinter, they have 24 hours of darkness.

Earth Facts

Extreme climates

● The Atacama Desert in Chile is the driest place on Earth. Some areas of the Atacama have had no rain for 400 years.

● The wettest place on Earth is Maghalaya State in northeast India, where almost 39 feet (12 meters) of rain falls every year.

e two photographs show the same woods during
summer and the winter in a temperate part of the
d.

Life on Earth

As far as we know, Earth is the only place in the Solar System where there is life. Earth supports a staggering variety of life, from microscopic bacteria to towering trees and giant whales.

Water and air

Life can only exist on Earth because there is liquid water. Animals also rely on oxygen in the atmosphere to breathe. Without water and the atmosphere, Earth would be as dry and lifeless as the Moon. Earth has liquid water because it is just the right distance from the Sun. If it were closer to the Sun, the water would boil and evaporate. If it were farther away from the Sun, the water would be frozen.

The biosphere

The biosphere is made up of all the places on Earth where life exists. It includes the ocean bottoms to mountain summits, rivers and lakes, soil, the surface, and the atmosphere.

Cacti are adapted t live in the desert, where they may get no water for many months.

Life thrives in the world's rain forests, where there is plenty of sunshine and rainfall.

 oceans are vast compared to the land. They make up 97 percent the biosphere. The biosphere is as big as it is, because forms of have adapted to survive in extreme conditions, such as those in polar ice caps and the ocean depths.

ergy for life

 the energy needed for animals and nts to grow and live comes from the Sun. nts use energy in sunlight to grow. They at the bottom of the food chain. Some mals eat the plants as food. Other mals eat these animals, and are in turn en by others.

e origins of life

 how do scientists think that life on Earth jan? Earth was formed about 4,600 lion years ago. About 4,000 million years , Earth looked very different from how it es today. It was covered in volcanoes that ught a mixture of chemicals to the face during eruptions. The chemicals mixed h water, forming pools. The chemicals in the pools reacted jether to form the complex chemicals that are the building blocks ife. These grouped together to form the very first, very simple ms of life.

Earth Facts

Life facts

● The chemical reactions that created the complex chemicals needed for life may have been set off by lightning strikes.

● None of the Earth's early forms of life exists today. In fact, 99 percent of all the life forms that have ever lived are extinct.

Formation of the Earth

Earth was formed at the same time that the Sun and other planets were formed, too. Earth began its life as a ball of hot rock with a molten surface.

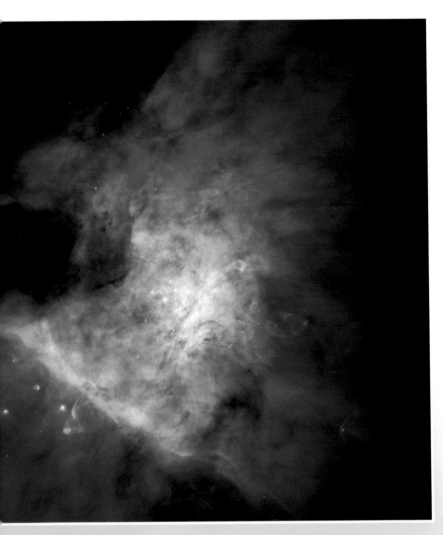

A nebula far out in space. It may form new solar systems in the distant future.

Birth of the Solar System

The whole of our Solar System formed from part of a vast cloud of gas and dust called a *nebula*. About 5 billion years ago, gravity made the gas and dust clump together very slowly and begin to spin. Then gravity made it collapse more quickly to form an extremely dense ball of material. Intense heat and pressure in the center of the ball started nuclear reactions. Energy from the reactions produced heat and light, so the ball began to shine. This was our Sun.

Planetesimals and planets

Scientists believe that the planets formed after the Sun, from a spinning disk of material left over after the Sun formed. This was made up of gas, dust, and small grains of rock. When bits of the rock and dust collided, they stuck together. Very slowly, gravity pulled these large pieces of rock together. Over thousands of years, boulders formed which are known as *planetesimals*. They were the building blocks of the planets. Eventually, gravity pulled the planetesimals together to form Earth and other planets.

Overall, it took 100 million years for Earth and other planets to form. The material left over from the formation of the Sun also formed the moons around the planets and all the other bits of the Solar System, such as asteroids and comets.

The early Earth

Earth began its life with a molten surface. The surface gradually cooled as heat escaped into space. Eventually it became solid. The space between the planets was filled with lumps of rock that bombarded their surfaces, smashing holes in them. These massive collisions created heat that kept Earth's surface hot. A really huge collision probably smashed off a piece of Earth, forming the Moon (see pages 26-27). Gradually the bombardment subsided. But the surface was still covered in volcanoes that spewed lava over the surface. You can find out how Earth has changed since on page 22.

Earth's rocks, such these in Yosemite tional Park, are rmed from materials at came from a bula.

Earth's Story

Earth was a very different place now than it was when it was formed 4,600 million years ago. Then there was no atmosphere, no oceans, no mountain ranges, no rivers, and no life. Over billions of years, Earth has transformed into the planet we know today.

The moving continents

Today Earth's crust is made up of giant tectonic plates (see page 9). These may have formed more than 2 billion years ago. They have been slowly moving ever since. Hundreds of millions of years ago, the continents were in completely different places from where they are today. For example, about 400 million years ago, Africa was at the South Pole.

This is how Earth looked about 250 million years ago. "supercontinent" i. known as Pangaea

Oceans and atmosphere

The water that now fills Earth's oceans, lakes, and rivers probably came from volcanoes. It came out as water vapor, then condensed in the air, forming clouds. Rain from the clouds gathered to form the oceans. Some of our water may have come from comets that collided with Earth.

Chemicals from the eruptions also formed the atmosphere. At first, the atmosphere was made up of carbon dioxide, water vapor, nitrogen, and other chemicals. There was no oxygen. The oxygen in today's atmosphere was given off by plants.

e-changing events

bombardment of rocks that hit Earth in its
ly life has almost stopped, but not
npletely. Meteorites do still hit Earth. In
past, large impacts have destroyed
ny species of animals and plants. A huge
teorite impact may have caused the
osaurs to die off.

mate change

world's climates have been changing
millions of years. For example, there
e been periods of cold, called *ice ages*,
en thick ice sheets covered much of
th. These changes took place over
usands or millions of years. Today,
temperature of the atmosphere is
nging so fast that scientists think
issions from burning fuels is the cause
e page 13).

How do we know?

Studying fossils

We know about the history of Earth
from its rocks. One way to tell the age of
a piece of rock is to look at the fossils in it.
Fossils are the remains of ancient plants and
animals. If a rock contains a fossil of a
particular plant or animal, geologists can tell
how old it is, because they know when the
plant or animal lived.

*A palaeontologist extracts a dinosaur fossil from
some rock. Without fossils, we would not know
that the dinosaurs ever existed.*

arth's early life, Earth would have
n covered in hundreds of craters like
one in Arizona.

The Changing Surface

Earth's surface is still changing today. The tectonic plates are moving slowly, a few inches a year. This movement builds up the landscape in places, and erosion wears it down again. These processes slowly change the surface, so features that were present millions of years ago no longer exist.

Lava flowing from volcanoes, such as one in the Philippi... forms new rock on Earth's surface.

Mountain building

Earth's mountains are built up where the edges of tectonic plates collide into each other. This crumples the layers of rock at one or both edges, pushing up mountain ranges. For example, the Himalayas were created when the Indian plate collided with the Eurasian plate. Mountains are also built up by volcanoes. Others are formed when molten rock rises underground, pushing up the surface above.

How do we know?

Remote sensing

We can see how Earth's surface is changing with the help of remote sensing satellites. The satellites take photographs, make three-dimensional maps, and take measurements of the surface and atmosphere. Many satellites have been launched to monitor the changes that human activities are causing to Earth, such as melting glaciers and the hole in the ozone layer (see page 13).

This photograph of Kazakhstan and the Caspian Sea was taken by the Envis... remote sensing satellite.

*he coasts, the
n of waves
ks up rocks,
ing coastal
ion. In other
es the coast is
up.*

Erosion

As fast as new mountains are built up, they are worn down again by erosion. The rocks are broken up in different ways. Repeated heating and cooling in the day and night makes rocks crack. Ice forming in cracks also breaks up rocks. Rocks are worn down by loose rock particles blowing in the wind. They are also broken up when they are hit by particles carried by flowing water, glaciers (slowly moving rivers of ice), and waves. Once rocks are broken up, they are carried downhill by flowing water and the wind. The particles of rock are called *sediment*. The sediment is deposited where a river flows across flat plains and at the sea. Over millions of years, whole mountain ranges are worn down and turned into layers of sediment.

The rock cycle

Old rocks are always being destroyed, and new rocks are continually being made. For example, old rocks are destroyed by erosion, and new rocks are made when molten rock flows from volcanoes, cools, and solidifies. Sediment slowly forms new rocks when it is buried deep underground.

The Moon

The Moon is Earth's only natural satellite (a satellite is an object that orbits another object). The Moon looks very different from Earth. It is covered with craters, it has no atmosphere or water, and no life. The Moon is kept in its orbit by gravity pulling Earth and Moon together.

Near and far

The Moon spins on its axis very slowly compared to Earth. It completes one spin every time it orbits Earth, so that the same side of the Moon faces Earth all the time. The Moon spins like this because Earth's gravity has locked one side of the Moon in place. We call this side of the Moon the *near side*. The opposite side of the Moon, called the *far side*, is always hidden from Earth. The only people who have seen the far side are the astronauts who have visited the Moon.

How the Moon formed

We know a lot about the Moon, but nobody is really sure how the Moon formed in the first place. Astronomers have suggested several theories.

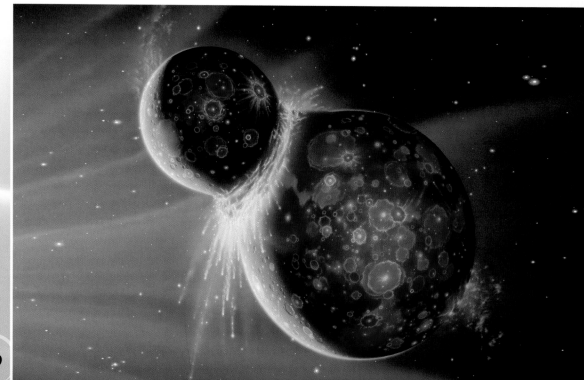

This is what the collision that create the Moon may ha looked like. Debris from the collision formed the Moon.

The Moon

Diameter: 2,155 mi. (3,476 km)

Mass: 80 billion billion tons

Density: 2.8 tons per cubic yard
            (3.3 tonnes/cubic meter)

Temperature in center of core: 2,732°F (1,500°C)

Surface temperature: -247°F to 221°F (-155°C to 105°C)

One is that Earth and Moon formed at the same time from the same cloud of rock and dust. Another is that the Moon drifted close to Earth and was captured in its orbit by Earth's gravity. But the most popular theory is that Earth was hit by a huge body, perhaps as big as Mars. This threw huge amounts of rock into space that came together to form the Moon.

Structure of the Moon

Like Earth, the Moon has a crust, a mantle, and a core. Unlike Earth, there are no tectonic plates and no volcanoes. This means that the Moon's surface does not change over time as Earth's surface does. This is why craters that were made by meteorite impacts hundreds of millions of years ago are still visible. Part of the Moon's core may be molten. Movements of the rock here may cause the "moonquakes" that have been recorded by instruments placed on the Moon's surface by astronauts and lunar probes.

The Moon seen from Earth. This side of the Moon always faces Earth.

Moon Rock

On Earth, new rocks are made and old rocks are destroyed all the time. This does not happen on the Moon. All of the Moon's rock is at least 3,000 million years old. It was formed when the Moon cooled and crusted over.

Weathering on the Moon

The Moon's surface is covered with a thick layer of dust, rock fragments, and boulders. This mixture is called regolith. It is formed as solid rock is broken up into dust by two types of weathering. The first is heat-cool weathering. This happens because the surface is heated to 221°F (105°C) and cooled to −247°F (−155°C) as parts of the Moon move in and out of sunlight. It makes the rocks expand and contract, which cracks them apart. The second form of weathering is called *space weathering*. This is caused by meteorite impacts that pulverize the rock. Most impacts are micrometeorites, less than .04 in. (1 mm) across, that travel up to 62,100 mph (100,000 kph).

The collisions that caused these hund
of craters smashed
Moon's rock into d

An astronaut from the Apollo 17 mission uses an adjustable scoop to collect samples of rock from the Moon's surface.

How do we know?

Collecting Moon rock

We know a great deal about the Moon's rocks from examining the rock samples brought back to Earth by the astronauts of the Apollo missions. Astronauts from the six Apollo missions brought back a total of 838 lb. (380 kg) of Moon rock. In 1970, the Soviet probe *Luna 16* automatically collected a sample of Moon dust and sent it back to Earth in a rocket-powered capsule.

ght and dark rocks

m Earth, we can see that the on's surface has light and dark as. These areas are formed from two erent types of rock. The lighter areas made mainly from a light-colored rock ed *anorthosite*, and the darker areas are de from dark-colored rock similar to basalt.

the Moon's surface cooled, the anorthosite floated to surface, cooled, and solidified, forming the Moon's crust. This pened more than 4,000 million years ago. The darker, basaltlike k was formed afterward, when molten rock leaked through the st and filled giant craters to form the Moon's seas. This pened between 4,000 million and 3,000 million years ago.

The Moon's Craters

The Moon's surface is littered with craters. They were formed by thousands of meteorites smashing into the Moon's surface at an incredibly high speed. Most craters were formed more than 3.5 billion years ago. The craters are still there because there is no erosion on the Moon to wear the surface down.

Bowls and saucers

The Moon's craters exist in a wide range of sizes, from mini-craters a few feet across, to giant craters hundreds of miles across. There were even larger craters in the Moon's early life. Some of them have been flooded by lava to form the Moon's seas (see page 32). The biggest impacts cracked the surface, forming features such as scarps (steep steps in the landscape). In many places, there are craters within craters, and in others, overlapping craters.

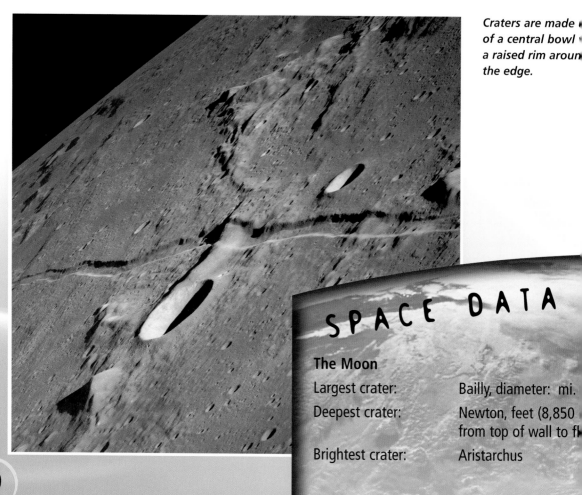

Craters are made of a central bowl a raised rim around the edge.

SPACE DATA

The Moon

Largest crater: Bailly, diameter: mi.

Deepest crater: Newton, feet (8,850 from top of wall to f

Brightest crater: Aristarchus

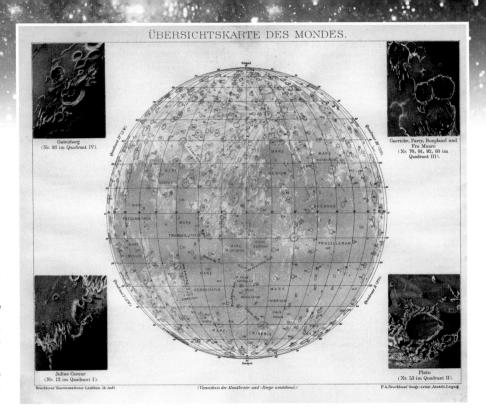

ÜBERSICHTSKARTE DES MONDES.

Gutenberg
(Nr. 93 im Quadrant IV).

Guericke, Parry, Bonpland und Fra Mauro
(Nr. 76, 91, 92, 93 im Quadrant III).

Julius Caesar
(Nr. 12 im Quadrant I).

Plato
(Nr. 53 im Quadrant II).

ap of the near side of the Moon. The craters are named ter famous people, such as the philosopher, Plato, and Gutenberg, the inventor.

Small impacts create simple, shallow, bowl-shaped craters, up to a few miles across. The surface rocks are thrown up to form a wall around the crater. Medium-sized impacts affect layers of rock deeper in the crust. These layers bounce back to form a central peak in a flat-bottomed, saucer-shaped crater. Massive impacts create giant explosions that throw up rings of mountains around and inside the crater. Surface rock is thrown thousands of miles outward.

Ray craters

A few of the Moon's craters are younger than the others. They were made by meteorites that hit the Moon after the bombardment in its early life died down. The material thrown outward by the impacts can still be seen as rays spreading out from the craters.

Space facts

Crater theories

● Until the middle of last century, many astronomers thought that the Moon's craters were the tops of volcanoes.

● During a full moon, you can see three of the brightest ray craters, Tycho, Copernicus, and Kepler.

More Surface Features

Craters are not the Moon's only features. The other main feature are huge dark regions known as *seas*. The Moon also has huge mountain ranges and wide canyons.

Seas

The Moon's seas are not really seas, because there is no liquid wa on the Moon. They were called seas because they looked like sea early astronomers. They are actually giant, flat-bottomed basins. The seas are the result of meteorite impacts in the early history o the Moon. These impacts created vast craters. Later, the craters flooded with molten rock that leaked from un the crust. The impacts that created the larger seas were extremel powerful. For example, t crater that formed the Mare Imbrium was over 620 miles (1,000 kilomete across.

The large, dark gray patches are the Moon's seas. You can see them easily from Earth.

Some of the lunar mountain range known as the Alps. The Alpine Valley cuts across it.

ountains and valleys

e Moon's mountains formed in a fferent way from those on Earth. :e the craters and seas, the Moon's ountain ranges were formed by pacts. They are made up of the aterial thrown outward by giant pacts. For example, the Montes enninus range runs along the edge the Mare Imbrium, and was formed the impact that created the sea. ere are also some canyons on the on. These were not formed by ter, but by flowing lava.

ar and far side

e near side and far side of the on are very different. The far side more craters than the near side, t it has only a few, very small seas. ronomers do not yet understand why se differences exist.

How do we know?

Trips to the far side

Astronomers have studied the near side of the Moon for thousands of years, but we had no idea what the far side looked like until 1959. That was the year that a probe, *Luna 3*, first went into orbit around the Moon, and sent photographs back to Earth. The first people to see the far side were the astronauts of *Apollo 8* in 1968, as the craft was tested for the Moon landings the following year.

The Luna 3 probe

Phases of the Moon

We see the Moon because light from the Sun bounces off of it. Th[e] Sun lights only one side of the Moon. The Moon seems to change shape from day to day because we see different parts of this lit side as the Moon moves around its orbit. These shapes are called the *phases of the Moon*.

The changing Moon

A crescent Moon is seen just before and just after a New Moon.

When the Moon is on the opposite side of Earth to the Sun, the Su[n] lights up the whole of the near side of the Moon, so we see a complete disk. This is called a *Full Moon*. When the Moon is on th[e] same side of Earth as the Sun, the Sun lights up the far side of the Moon. Non[e] of the near side is lit, so th[e] Moon is dark. This is calle[d] a *New Moon*.

Between the New Moon and the Full Moon, we se[e] different amounts of the [lit] side. A few days after a New Moon we see a thin slice of Moon, called a *Crescent Moon*. A few day[s] later, we can see half a Moon. A few days after this, we see three-quarter[s] of a Moon, called a *Gibbo[us] Moon*. Then we see the F[ull] Moon. After the Full Moo[n] the Moon's lit part gradually gets smaller again, until we see the N[ew] Moon again. The whole process, between one Ne[w] Moon and the next, take[s] an average of 29.5 days. This is called a *lunar mon[th]*

...les

...gravitational pull of
...Moon causes the tides
...he oceans on Earth.
...Moon pulls the water
...the nearest side of
...th into a bulge several
...t high. A bulge also
...ns on the opposite
...e of Earth. The bulges
...y still as Earth spins
...derneath them. A place
...Earth moves through
...o bulges a day, making
...tide rise and fall twice
...ay. The Sun's gravity
...o affects the tides. The
...hest and lowest tides
...pen when the Sun and
...on are in line with
...h other. This occurs on
...days of the New
...on and Full Moon.

This composite photograph shows the phases of the Moon, from one New Moon to another.

Earth Fact

Highest tides

● The largest tidal range in the world happens in the Bay of Fundy, Canada. At high tide, sea level is 52 feet (16 meters) higher than at low tide.

Eclipses

A shadow forms where an object blocks out light. Earth makes a shadow in space on the opposite side of Earth to the Sun. The Moon makes a shadow, too. Sometimes the movements of Earth, the Moon and the Sun bring them all into line. Then the Moon casts a shadow on Earth, or Earth casts a shadow on the Moon. These events are called *eclipses*.

Solar eclipses

A solar eclipse happens when the Moon casts a shadow on Earth. The Moon's shadow is much smaller than Earth, so it makes a dark spot on Earth's surface. The shadow has a dark center, called the *umbra*, and a lighter edge, called the *penumbra*. The Moon's movement along its orbit, and Earth's spin, make the shadow move across the surface.

A partial eclipse happens when part of the Sun is blocked out by the Moon.

When the dark central shadow moves over a place on Earth's surface, people there see a total eclipse of the Sun. From Earth, the Moon and Sun appear to be almost the same size, and during a total eclipse, the Moon just covers the Sun. Then it turns dark, like night, and the temperature drops. It takes a few minutes for the shadow to sweep past.

Total eclipses happen only every few years. Partial eclipses are more common. These happen when the outer, lighter shadow of the Moon passes over places on Earth. The Sun is not completely covered, but the Moon appears to take a bite out of it.

Moon seen from ~~h~~ during a lunar ~~~se~~. The top is still ~~y~~ the Sun.

Total eclipses of the Sun are useful events for astronomers. The Moon blocks out the brightness of the Sun's light, allowing them to study the Sun's outer atmosphere.

Never look directly at the Sun, with or without binoculars or a telescope, even during an eclipse. It could seriously damage your eyes.

Lunar eclipses

A lunar eclipse happens when the Earth casts a shadow on the Moon. It only happens when there is a full Moon, when Earth is directly between the Sun and Moon. A lunar eclipse makes all or part of the Moon disappear in darkness.

SPACE DATA

Future total solar eclipses

Date	Where visible
August 2008	Canada, Greenland, Siberia, Mongolia, China
July 2009	India, Nepal, China, Central Pacific
July 2010	South Pacific, Easter Island, Chile, Argentina

How we Observe Earth and its Moon

Our knowledge of Earth, the Moon, and the rest of the Solar Sys has come from making observations from Earth and from space, from sending astronauts and spacecraft to explore space. You ca out about exploration on page 40.

Telescopes

The main way of observing the Moon (and other objects in spa from Earth is by using optical telescopes. An optical telescope makes distant objects appear larger, so that we can see mor detail in the objects than we can see with the naked eye. Optical telescopes work by collecting light coming from a object and focusing it to form an image of the object. There are two main types of telescope. A *refracting telescope* uses a lens to collect and focus the ligh *reflecting telescope* uses a mirror instead. The larger the mirror or lens, the more light that ca be collected, and the more detail that can be se in an object. Most astronomers use reflecting telescopes, because they give clearer images an because large mirrors are easier to make than large lenses.

The image made by a telescope's lens or mir viewed with an eyepiece, which works like magnifying glass. Astronomers also use electronic detectors, like the chips ir digital cameras, that record the image, so that it can be viewed processed by a computer.

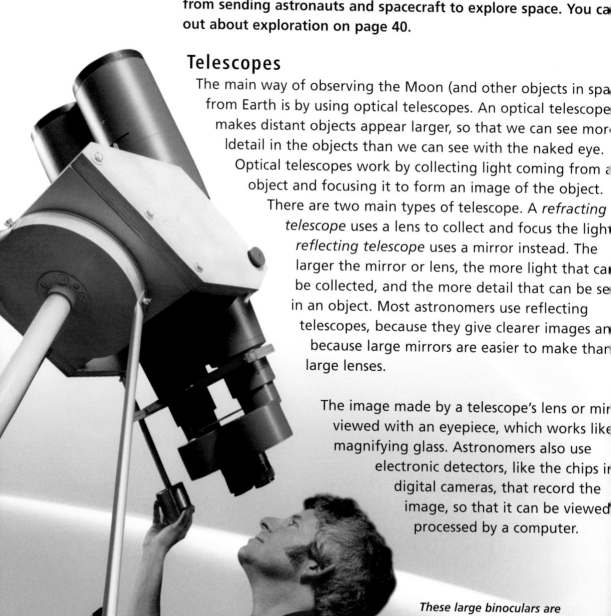

These large binoculars are made up of two telescopes. They are excellent for studying the Moon.

Remote sensing

Much of what we know about Earth has been learned by observations that scientists have made on the surface. But our knowledge has been widened by making observations from satellites above Earth. From their orbits, these satellites can see a wide area of Earth's surface. The satellites carry a wide variety of sensors. These sensors detect light and other forms of radiation, such as infrared and ultraviolet, coming from Earth, and send their data back to Earth by radio. Using satellites like this is called *remote sensing*. Remote sensing is used to study the atmosphere, the oceans, and the land. For example, satellites measure the level of different gases in the atmosphere above the globe, the speed of ocean currents, and the type of vegetation on the surface.

Large optical telescopes are sited on mountain tops, so that they are less likely to be affected by cloud cover.

Earth Facts

Telescope records

● The largest telescope mirrors in the world are in the twin Keck telescopes, in Hawaii. Each is 33 feet (10 meters) across.

● The latest research telescopes have mirrors that change shape all the time to remove the distortion of images caused by the Earth's atmosphere.

How we Explore Earth and its Moon

Looking through telescopes can only tell us a certain amount abo[ut]
our Solar System. And it can't tell us anything about the places [where we]
can't see, such as the far side of the Moon. To find out more, we[?]
have to visit them, or send space probes to them, and that mean[s]
going into space.

Getting into space

Space is only a few hundred miles away, but it is extremely hard [to]
get there because of Earth's gravity. If a spacecraft simply went
straight up and then switched off its engines, it would fall straigh[t]
back to Earth. Instead, spacecraft aim to go into orbit at high spe[ed]
a few hundred miles above Earth. Their high speed means that th[ey]
don't fall back to Earth, but circle it instead.

A rocket lifts off. About nine-tenths of its weight is made up of fuel for the engines.

The speed a spacecraft must reach to stay in orbit is 17,360 mph
(28,000 kph). That's about 30 times faster than a jet airliner. Any
slower, and the spacecraft would lose altitude again. Spacecraft n[eed]
an enormous push to lift them into orbit and to reach orbital spe[ed]

They need extremely powerful launch vehicles, such as rockets and space shuttles. Their rocket engines produce huge thrust and also work in space, where there is no air.

After a vertical liftoff, a rocket gains height and then gradually tilts further to one side. When it reaches space, it is flying parallel to Earth's surface.

Probes

Probes are unmanned spacecraft that visit other planets. To leave Earth's orbit and travel into the Solar System, a probe must travel even faster—about 24,800 miles per hour (40,000 kilometers per hour). This allows it to escape Earth's gravity. Once the probes are up to this speed, they can switch off their engines. There is no air in space to slow them down again. Some probes are designed to orbit or land on other planets. They have to slow down again to drop into orbit or descend to the surface.

A's CloudSat erimental satellite le to observe ds from space and l back information ut precipitation. dSat was carried orbit in 2006 by a a II rocket.

Manned space flights

Sending astronauts out into the Solar System is much more difficult than sending probes. The astronauts have to take everything they need with them, including air and water. Their spacecraft must protect them from the harmful radiation in space and from the intense heat of the Sun. They also have to return the astronauts safely to Earth. These difficulties are why the Moon is the only place in the Solar System that astronauts have visited.

The Future

A human lifetime lasts for a blink of an eye in the life of Earth. Earth as we know it is just a phase in its billions of years of history. Earth was very different in the past, and it will be very different in the future. So how will it change?

Climate change

Earth's climates have been changing slowly for millions of years, and they will continue to change. There will be periods when the Earth is warmer and periods when it is cooler. There may be more ice ages. The important questions at the moment is how much our activities will affect the climate over the next few hundred years, how we can reduce these effects, and how will we adapt to the changes.

Surface changes

The world's glaciers are slowly melting as Earth's climate changes. They may eventually disappear altogether.

The processes that shape Earth's surface will continue. Over millions of years, the world's mountain ranges will be eroded, and other mountains will be pushed up. The continents will gradually move from their current positions, and someday a giant supercontinent may form again.

n the other hand, the Moon will still ook as it does today, but maybe with n extra crater or two. And scientists re predicting that some time in the uture, Earth will probably be hit by a rge meteorite, creating a giant ater. This would destroy much of the anet's surface, cause enormous arthquakes and tsunamis, and fill the mosphere with dust for years.

A hydrothermal vent on the ocean floor. We have only explored a tiny fraction of the ocean depths.

arth's end

about 5,000 million years, the Sun will run out of fuel. will grow into a red ball of hot gas, so large that it will swallow the inner planets, destroying Earth and its oon.

uture exploration

ere on Earth, scientists are still trying to derstand why tectonic plates move, and how predict earthquakes and volcanoes. They are o trying to understand what exactly causes anges to Earth's climates. In the future, more mote-sensing satellites will help them.

en though we are sending space probes to e moons of other planets, there is still a eat deal to find out about Earth's Moon. veral missions are planned to map the face and study rocks and moonquakes.

SA (the National Aeronautics & Space Administration) plans to d astronauts to the Moon by 2020. It is designing a new acecraft, the *Crew Exploration Vehicle*, for the task. Space probes currently looking for suitable lunar landing sites. Missions may t the Moon's poles, where the Sun shines almost all the time, and ere there may be ice that can be melted for drinking water.

Space Fact

● The Moon is slowly drifting away from the Earth by a few inches a year, so the Moon will look smaller in the sky in the far future. Since one of the Moon's effects on the Earth is to lengthen the day, this means that days will be longer in future, too.

Timeline of Discovery

1609   Thomas Harriot uses a telescope to draw the first accurate map of the Moon.

1840   The first photograph of the Moon is taken.

1915   Alfred Wegener proposes the theory of plate tectonics.

1919   During a solar eclipse, it is proved that the Sun's gravity bends light slightly, as suggested by Einstein's theory of relativity.

1946   Radar is used to measure the exact distance to the Moon.

1959   *Luna 1* is the first probe to fly past the Moon.

1959   The probe *Luna 3* is the first probe to fly around the Moon. It sends back the first photographs of the far side of the Moon.

1960   The first weather satellite, *TIROS 1*, is launched.

This is the lunar module of the Apollo spacecraft, which carried astronauts down to the Moon's surface

1964   The first Nimbus remote-sensing satellite is launched for studying the oceans and atmosphere.

1966   *Luna 9* is the first probe to make a successful landing on the Moon.

1968   *Apollo 8* carries astronauts on their first orbit of the Moon.

Astronaut Neil Armstrong stands on the Moon's surface.

1969 Astronauts land on the Moon for the first time aboard *Apollo 11*. Neil Armstrong becomes the first person to step onto the Moon's surface.

1970 The first lunar rover, *Lunokhod 1*, lands on the Moon.

1971 Astronauts from *Apollo 15* use a buggy to explore the Moon's surface.

1972 *Apollo 17* is the last manned mission to visit the Moon.

1972 The first Landsat satellite, *ERTS 1*, is launched to photograph and study the Earth's surface.

1998 *Lunar Prospector* orbits the Moon, and finds evidence of water ice in craters.

2004 President Bush announces a new plan to send astronauts to the Moon.

2004 The Aura satellite is launched to study the ozone layer.

Glossary

asteroid A rocky object that orbits the Sun, but that is not large enough to be a planet. Most asteroids orbit between the orbits of Mars and Jupiter.

astronaut A person who travels into space, to carry out scientific experiments, or to operate a spacecraft.

astronomer A scientist who studies planets, moons, and other objects in space.

atmosphere A layer of gas that surrounds a planet or moon.

comet A small, icy object that orbits the Sun.

condense To turn from gas to liquid.

continent A large land mass on Earth (there are currently seven continents).

crater A dish-shaped hole in the surface of a planet or moon, created by an object from space smashing into the surface.

crust The solid, outer layer of the Earth.

erosion The gradual wearing down of the landscape by the weather and flowing water.

evaporate To turn from liquid to gas.

far side The side of the Moon that faces away from Earth.

glacier A river of ice that flows slowly down from an ice-covered mountain range.

global warming The gradual warming of Earth's atmosphere, caused by the atmosphere trapping increasing amounts of heat from the Sun.

gravity A force that attracts all objects to each other.

hydrothermal vent A place on the ocean floor where hot water emerges from rocks underneath.

lunar To do with the Moon.

meteorite A rocky particle from space th crashes into the surface of a planet or moon.

moon An object that orbits around a planet, but that is not part of a planet's rings.

near side The side of the Moon that fac Earth.

nuclear reaction When the nucleus of a atom splits apart, or loses or gains some particles.

orbit 1) Moving around the Sun or a planet; 2) The path that an object takes it moves around the Sun or a planet.

ozone A gas that is a special form of oxygen (each particle is made up of thre oxygen atoms instead of the usual two).

ozone layer A layer of ozone gas high in Earth's atmosphere.

planet An object in space that orbits around the Sun, but that is not part of a large group of objects, such as asteroids comets.

probe A spacecraft launched into space send back information about the Sun, other planets, or moons.

satellite A spacecraft that orbits around the Earth.

tectonic plate One of the giant pieces th Earth's crust is broken into.

tsunami A high-speed wave that travels across the oceans, caused by an earthquake, volcano, or landslide.

water vapor The gas form of water, ma when liquid water boils.

urther Information

oks

Planets
id McNab and James Younger
Worldwide, 1999

ional Geographic Encyclopedia of Space
da K. Glover
ional Geographic Society, 2005

janizations

ional Aeronautics & Space
ministration (NASA)
anization that runs the US space
gram
w.nasa.gov

rnational Astronomical Union (IAU)
official world astronomy organization,
oonsible for naming stars, planets,
ons, and other objects in space
w.iau.org

Propulsion Laboratory (JPL)
ter responsible for NASA's robot space
bes
w.jpl.nasa.gov

opean Space Agency (ESA)
anization responsible for space flight
exploration of European countries
w.esa.int

The Planetary Society
Organization devoted to the exploration of
the Solar System
www.planetary.org

Web sites

Due to the changing nature of Internet links, The Rosen Publishing Group, Inc., has developed an online list of Web sites related to the subject of this book. This site is updated regularly. Please use this link to access the list:
www.rosenlinks.com/eas/earth/

Index

Numbers in **bold** indicate pictures.